W9-CIH-502

HUMANS IN SPACE

RACE INTO SPACE

DAVID JEFFERIS AND MAT IRVINE

Crabtree Publishing Company

www.crabtreebooks.com

Introduction

This is the story of how rocket pioneers made it possible to fly into space. There is no actual place where space starts because the air simply thins out the higher you go. International regulations declare anyone who flies higher than the Karman Line, which is 62 miles (100 kilometers) above the Earth, is an astronaut.

The first human to fly into space was Yuri Gagarin, a cosmonaut, or Russian astronaut, who circled the Earth in 1961. With the dawn of private space flight, the door to space is opening to almost anyone who is physically fit and can afford a ticket.

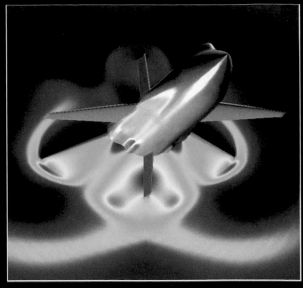

Crabtree Publishing Company
PMB 16A,
350 Fifth Avenue, Suite 3308
New York, NY 10118

616 Welland Avenue,
St. Catharines, Ontario
L2M 5V6

Coordinating Editor: Ellen Rodger
Editors: L. Michelle Nielsen, Carrie Gleason
Production Coordinator: Rose Gowsell
Prepress technician: Nancy Johnson

© 2007 Crabtree Publishing Company

Educational advisor:
Julie Stapleton
Written and produced by:
David Jefferis and Mat Irvine/Buzz Books

©2007 David Jefferis/Buzz Books

Library of Congress
Cataloging-in-Publication Data

Jefferis, David.
  Race into space / written by David Jefferis & Mat Irvine.
    p. cm. — (Humans in space)
  Includes index.
  ISBN-13: 978-0-7787-3102-3 (rlb)
  ISBN-10: 0-7787-3102-2 (rlb)
  ISBN-13: 978-0-7787-3116-0 (pb)
  ISBN-10: 0-7787-3116-2 (pb)
  1. Space race—United States—History—20th century—Juvenile literature.
  2. Space race—Soviet Union—History—20th century—Juvenile literature.
  I. Irvine, Mat. II. Title. III. Series.

TL793.J43 2007
629.45009'045—dc22

2007003462

Pictures from below, clockwise:
1   An early **space walk**, in 1965.
2   Computer image of air patterns around an X-15 rocket plane.
3   A Russian Soyuz rocket.
4   Climbing to space.
5   The White Knight carrier plane with SpaceShipOne underneath.

Contents

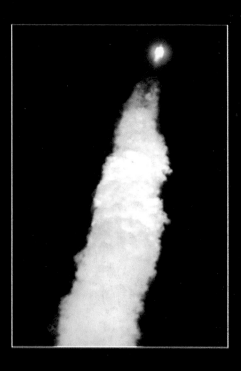

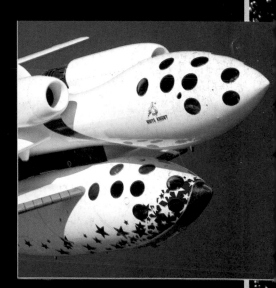

Leaving planet Earth

No human had left Earth until the 1960s, when space flight changed from a dream of the future to a reality.

The pull of **gravity**, or the force of attraction between objects, is what stops Earth's **atmosphere** from drifting off into space. Gravity keeps everything, including people, firmly on the ground. It is also the force that made space flight so difficult to achieve.

Soaring to the Karman Line, 62 miles (100 kilometers) up, is difficult, but reaching **orbit** requires a spacecraft to use even more energy. The spacecraft must move at about 17,500 miles per hour (28,000 kilometers per hour), otherwise it will fall back to Earth. Building rockets that could reach this speed made space travel possible.

Tsiolkovsky's rocket designs

▲ Russian scientist Konstantin Tsiolkovsky worked on many space flight problems in the early 1900s.

Spacecraft above the Earth

A flight to the Karman Line follows the path shown here (1) to scale with the Earth. Most crewed spacecraft orbit the Earth at more than twice this height (2). Uncrewed spacecraft, such as the **Hubble Space Telescope** (HST), often move in higher orbits (3). The HST's orbit is shown in the circle (far left).

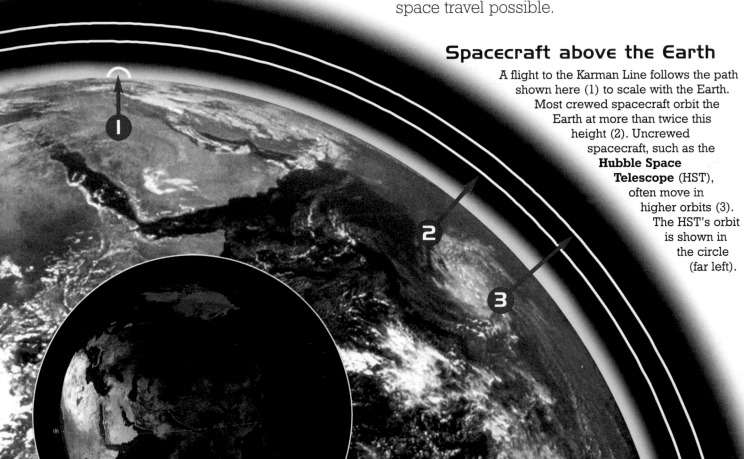

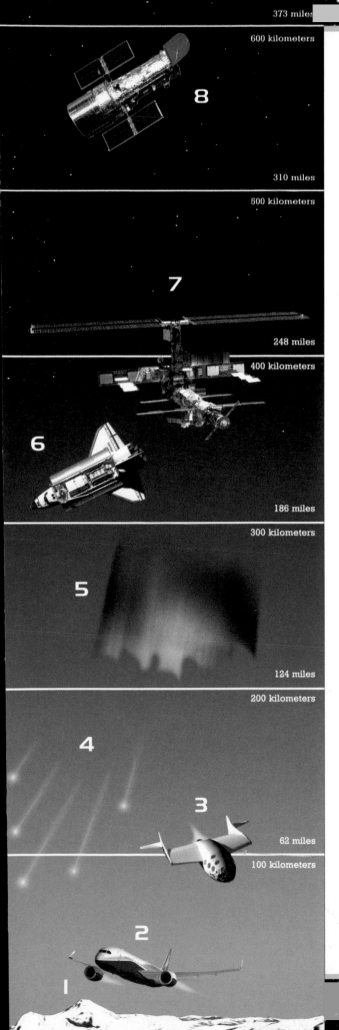

373 miles
600 kilometers

8

310 miles
500 kilometers

7

248 miles
400 kilometers

6

186 miles
300 kilometers

5

124 miles
200 kilometers

4

3

62 miles
100 kilometers

2

1

G-forces

G-force is the term used to describe the acceleration of gravity. On the ground, Earth's gravity pulls at objects with a force of 1 G. If a person goes in a high-speed elevator, they can feel the extra force as it speeds up.

In the early days of space flight, many tests were carried out to see what astronauts could withstand. The record stands at 46.2 G.

Reality is not quite as tough. The Soyuz rocket (right) accelerates at just 4 G for the first two minutes of takeoff.

A volunteer is subjected to many times the force of gravity

Space has no real "beginning" – the air just gets thinner as the distance from Earth increases. The Karman Line marks the "edge" of space. Artificial **satellites** cruise higher than the Karman Line. Earth's natural satellite and nearest neighbor in space, the Moon, is 239,000 miles (384,000 kilometers) away.

◀ The atmosphere is only thick enough for humans to breathe up to about 6.2 miles (10 kilometers).
1   Mount Everest is the highest point on Earth, at 5.5 miles (8.9 kilometers).
2   Jetliners usually cruise at up to 7.7 miles (12.5 kilometers).
3   The Karman Line lies at the edge of space. In 2004 the first private spacecraft flew above it.
4   **Meteors** are chunks of space rock. They hit the atmosphere at up to 37 miles per second (60 kilometers per second).
5   **Auroras** are glowing particles in the upper atmosphere.
6   Crewed craft orbit at about 200 to 400 miles (320 to 650 kilometers) up.

7   The crewed **International Space Station** (ISS) orbits at a height of about 218 miles (350 kilometers).
8   The uncrewed Hubble Space Telescope was placed in orbit by astronauts flying in a **Space Shuttle**. The HST orbits at 358 miles (575 kilometers).

RACEFACT
Space is a near-perfect **vacuum**, with no air to breathe. There are, however, enough particles to slow a spacecraft a little. From time to time, the International Space Station needs a small rocket boost to nudge it back up to its correct height.

Rocket pioneer

Long before the first rockets left the Earth, scientists had worked hard to make the dream of space flight a reality.

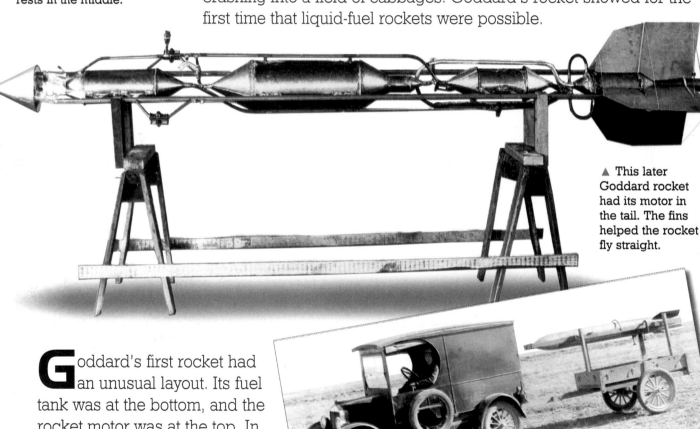

▲ Robert Goddard holds the launch structure of his first rocket. The rocket (arrowed) rests in the middle.

American rocket pioneer Robert Goddard developed the world's first **liquid-fuel rocket**. He launched his spidery-looking contraption in 1926, from farmland in Massachusetts, U.S. The rocket made a short flight, lasting less than three seconds, before crashing into a field of cabbages. Goddard's rocket showed for the first time that liquid-fuel rockets were possible.

▲ This later Goddard rocket had its motor in the tail. The fins helped the rocket fly straight.

Goddard's first rocket had an unusual layout. Its fuel tank was at the bottom, and the rocket motor was at the top. In later designs, Goddard changed this layout to the one we know today, with a motor at the bottom and fuel tanks and cargo above.

Goddard developed more rockets throughout the 1920s and 1930s. Today, he has a crater on the Moon named after him.

▲ Goddard's small truck tows a rocket to a launch site.

► Rockets work much like a balloon. A rush of gases shoot at high speed out of a nozzle causing the rocket to move in the opposite direction.

◄ One of the most powerful liquid-fuel engines used today is the Russian RD-180, which can supply 584 tons (530 tonnes) of **thrust**. The most powerful liquid-fuel engine ever made was the F-1, which was first test-fired in 1959. Later F-1s gave up to 783 tons (710 tonnes) of thrust, and were used to power huge U.S. Saturn rockets.

RACEFACT

Isaac Newton's Third Law of Motion, published in 1687, explains how rockets work. The "action" of the high-speed exhaust out of the engine nozzle is balanced by an equal "reaction" in the opposite direction, causing the rocket to move forward.

Liquid-fuel rocket motor

Liquid or solid rockets?

Solid-fuel rockets work in a similar way to fireworks. Once switched on, they give full power, but cannot stop until their fuel is used up.

Liquid-fuel rockets are more useful. They can be stopped and started in flight, and for many the power can be varied, like the accelerator on an automobile.

Solid-fuel rockets can come in useful though. The U.S. Space Shuttle (right) uses a pair of them for a two-minute power boost at liftoff from the launch pad. When empty, these **booster rockets** are dropped and parachute down to the sea, for re-use on later flights.

Solid-fuel rocket booster

V-2 and beyond

The first successful long-range rocket was the bullet-shaped V-2, a wartime terror weapon.

◀▶ By using a transporter called a Meillerwagen, which could haul heavy rockets, a V-2 could be launched almost anywhere. It could be set up, fueled, and launched in less than two hours.

▼ Most rockets built since the V-2 have followed its design.

Wernher von Braun was a German rocket enthusiast who experimented with liquid-fuel rockets in the 1920s. Later he showed his ideas to the German army, which gave him backing to develop his rockets further.

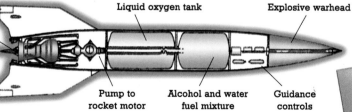

Rocket motor

Liquid oxygen tank

Explosive warhead

Pump to rocket motor

Alcohol and water fuel mixture

Guidance controls

Before long, von Braun's rockets were being test-fired successfully. These flights led to the construction of the V-2, one of the most advanced weapons of **World War II**. By late 1944, thousands of V-2s were being made. Many V-2s targeted Belgium and Britain, and carried 1.1 tons (1 tonne) of high explosives.

▲ Von Braun had plans for an advanced V-2. It had wings and room for a pilot, but was never built.

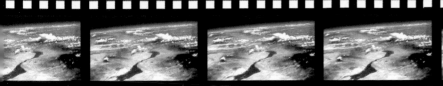

RACEFACT
The V-2 steered with eight rudders. Four of them adjusted the angle of the flame roaring out of the rocket motor. Four more rudders were on the fins. The V-2 flew faster than sound, so no one could hear it coming. The V-2 was not very accurate.

Early research rockets took movies of the Earth far below them

Wac-Corporal mounted on top of V-2

V-2 rocket

◀ Project Bumper's highest flight was made in February 1949, from a desert base in New Mexico, U.S. The rocket reached a record height of 250 miles (400 kilometers) above the Earth.

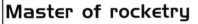

Master of rocketry

Wernher von Braun's team of rocket scientists worked on space projects that eventually allowed humans to fly to and land on the Moon.

In the early 1950s, von Braun showed what could be done, in the pages of the magazine *Collier's*. The color pictures showed readers von Braun's amazing vision of the future, with **space planes**, space stations, and missions to the Moon and Mars. Many of these ideas came true in later years, though humans have not yet visited Mars.

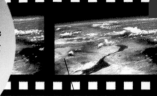

After World War II ended, von Braun went to work in the United States. In Project Bumper, they added a small Wac-Corporal rocket to a V-2, allowing it to fly even higher. In May 1948, Bumper's first rocket reached a height of nearly 80 miles (130 kilometers).

The March 1952 cover of *Collier's* showed a von Braun space plane

Stage rockets

The key to space flight was to build rockets made up of throwaway stages. When the fuel in a stage is used up, the stage falls off and the next stage takes over.

The rockets used for Project Bumper showed that multi-stage launchers worked well. Project Bumper used two stages, a modified V-2 and a Wac-Corporal rocket. When the V-2's fuel was used up, it fell away and the smaller Wac-Corporal took over, using its own fuel and rocket motor to go higher. This is the way that space rockets have been made since, though there have been many different designs.

▲ The Gemini 4 crewed spacecraft was launched by the two-stage Titan 2 rocket in 1965. In all, ten crewed Gemini missions were flown.

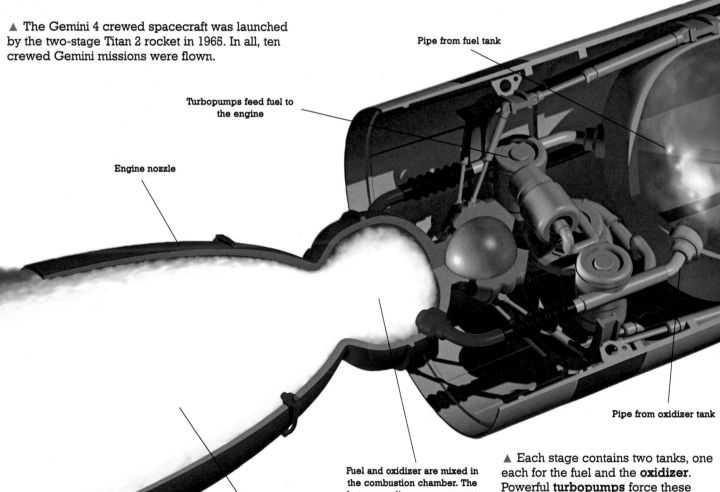

Pipe from fuel tank

Turbopumps feed fuel to the engine

Engine nozzle

Pipe from oxidizer tank

Fuel and oxidizer are mixed in the combustion chamber. The hot, expanding gases roar out of the engine nozzle

Expanding exhaust gases

▲ Each stage contains two tanks, one each for the fuel and the **oxidizer**. Powerful **turbopumps** force these fluids into the **combustion chamber**, where they are mixed and ignited. The flaming gases roar out of the bell-shaped engine nozzle.

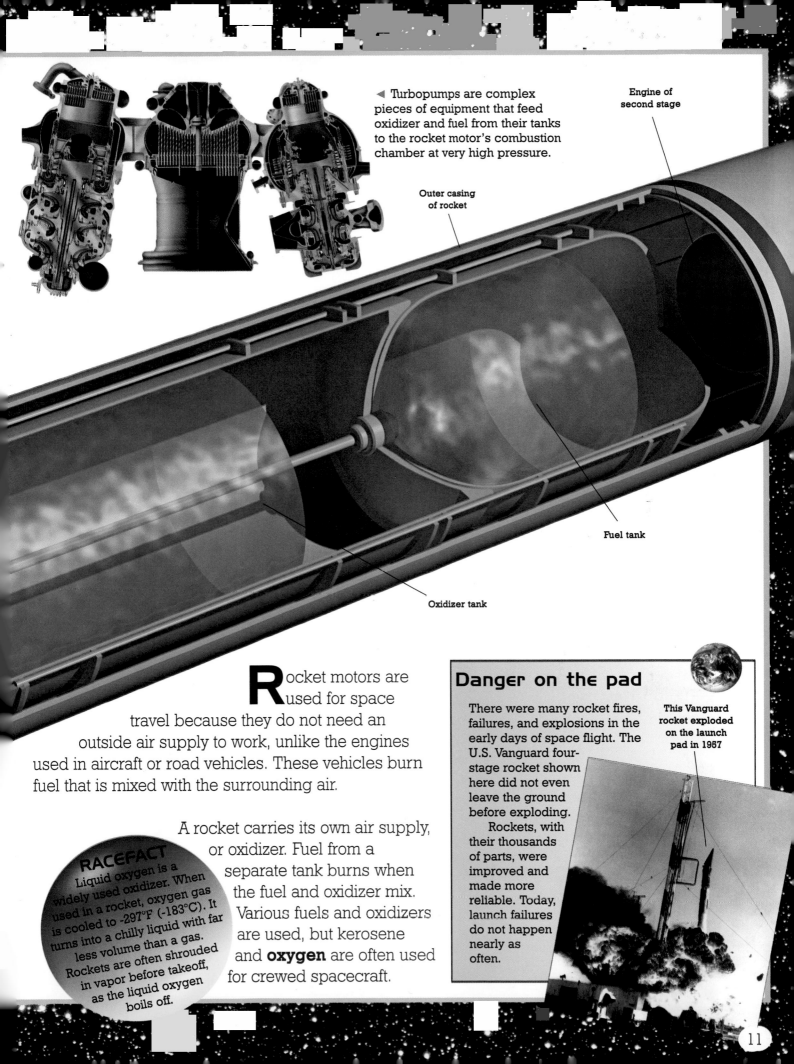

◄ Turbopumps are complex pieces of equipment that feed oxidizer and fuel from their tanks to the rocket motor's combustion chamber at very high pressure.

Engine of second stage

Outer casing of rocket

Fuel tank

Oxidizer tank

Rocket motors are used for space travel because they do not need an outside air supply to work, unlike the engines used in aircraft or road vehicles. These vehicles burn fuel that is mixed with the surrounding air.

A rocket carries its own air supply, or oxidizer. Fuel from a separate tank burns when the fuel and oxidizer mix. Various fuels and oxidizers are used, but kerosene and **oxygen** are often used for crewed spacecraft.

RACEFACT
Liquid oxygen is a widely used oxidizer. When used in a rocket, oxygen gas is cooled to -297°F (-183°C). It turns into a chilly liquid with far less volume than a gas. Rockets are often shrouded in vapor before takeoff, as the liquid oxygen boils off.

Danger on the pad

There were many rocket fires, failures, and explosions in the early days of space flight. The U.S. Vanguard four-stage rocket shown here did not even leave the ground before exploding.
Rockets, with their thousands of parts, were improved and made more reliable. Today, launch failures do not happen nearly as often.

This Vanguard rocket exploded on the launch pad in 1957

11

First humans in space

The first human to fly in orbit was Russian cosmonaut Yuri Gagarin in 1961. Others soon followed, including the first woman cosmonaut, Valentina Tereshkova.

▲ Vostok 1 takes off, with Gagarin inside.

The 1950s and 1960s were times of international competition between the United States and the **Soviet Union**, a group of states that included Russia. Both the United States and the Soviet Union wanted to be the first to make achievements in space. This became known as the "space race."

At first, the Soviet Union led the way, and in 1957 sent the first satellite, Sputnik 1, into space. This was a great shock to the Americans, and to Wernher von Braun and his team. A bigger shock lay ahead.

◄ Valentina Tereshkova became the first woman in space in 1963. Her flight in Vostok 6 lasted for nearly three days, during which she circled the Earth 48 times.

▲ Yuri Gagarin was 27 years old when he became the first human in space.

Rear equipment module

Communications antenna

RACEFACT
Sergei Korolev was the Soviet Union's space chief during the space race years. His identity was kept a secret though, and he was known for many years only as the "Chief Designer." Vostok and many other Soviet spacecraft all resulted from his work.

Russian cosmonaut Yuri Gagarin went into the record books when he became the first human to go into orbit. Just as Sputnik 1 had been a big surprise, so was Gagarin's flight. The United States space program went into overdrive to catch up.

► The Vostok capsule was a two-**module** design. The front **re-entry** module carried Gagarin and the flight controls. The controls were automatic, though Gagarin could take over in an emergency. The rear module held equipment and **braking rockets** to slow Vostok down for re-entry.

Fame across the world

Gagarin's flight was headline news all around the world, and he was honored in his own country for the achievement.

Coins were made in his name, and postage stamps with his picture were issued.

Many Russian streets, squares, and parks were named after him. Seven years after his flight, the Russian city of Gzhatsk was renamed Gagarin.

Today, cosmonauts who fly in Russian spacecraft are trained at the Gagarin Centre in Star City. Star City was specially built, with its own shops and railway station, and is not far from Moscow, Russia's capital city.

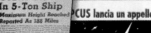

l'Unità
ORGANO DEL PARTITO COMUNISTA ITALIANO

L'U.R.S.S. IN DELIRIO - IL ATTONITO: UN UOMO SO____CO HA VINTO LO SPAZIO COSMICO

IL COMPAGNO YURI ___NTA IL VIAGGIO

PCUS lancia un appello

The Huntsville Times

Man Enters Space

'So Close, Yet So Far,' Sighs Cape

U.S. Had Hoped For Own Launch

Soviet Officer Orbits Globe In 5-Ton Ship

Maximum Height Reached Reported As 188 Miles

To Keep Up, U.S.A. Must Beat Like Hell

Avanza l'Uomo

Air for breathing was carried in storage bottles

Ball-shaped re-entry module

▲ The return from space nearly turned into a disaster when the re-entry module tumbled and would not separate from the equipment module (1). Gagarin did not stay in the capsule all the way down. Instead, he used a jet fighter-style ejector seat to leave the capsule in mid-air (2) using his own parachute (3) to land safely.

Hatch through which Gagarin ejected

Re-entry module covered in protective material for the return to Earth

▶ The re-entry capsule made a rough landing under large parachutes. The capsule was a sphere 7.5 feet (2.3 meters) across, weighing nearly 2.8 tons (2.5 tonnes).

Mercury flights

The United States followed up Gagarin's record-breaking flight by launching the single-seat Mercury spacecraft just a few weeks later.

The rockets being developed in the United States were smaller than the Soviet Union's Vostok. At launch the Mercury spacecraft weighed only about two tons (1.8 tonnes). The first flight was powered by a Redstone rocket, which blasted off just 23 days after Gagarin's flight.

◀ Alan Shepard Jr. (top) and John Glenn (left) were two members of the Mercury astronaut team.

▶ Astronauts called themselves "spam in a can" after a brand of canned meat.

The first American astronaut was Alan Shepard Jr., who made a 116 mile (187 kilometer) up-and-down flight above the Karman Line. In 1962, a bigger Atlas rocket blasted John Glenn into orbit. For the rest of the 1960s, Soviet and American scientists developed bigger and better spacecraft. Their goal: to be first to the Moon.

The X-15

Three X-15 rocket planes were built in the 1960s to explore the upper atmosphere. To fly a mission, an X-15 was flown off the ground by a carrier plane. Once high in the air, it was dropped, and the pilot fired a rocket motor. Plans were made for a high-power X-15 that could fly into orbit, but the simpler Mercury spacecraft replaced it.

▲ X-15 pilots wore astronaut-style suits.

▲ The X-15 was carried by a B-52 jet.

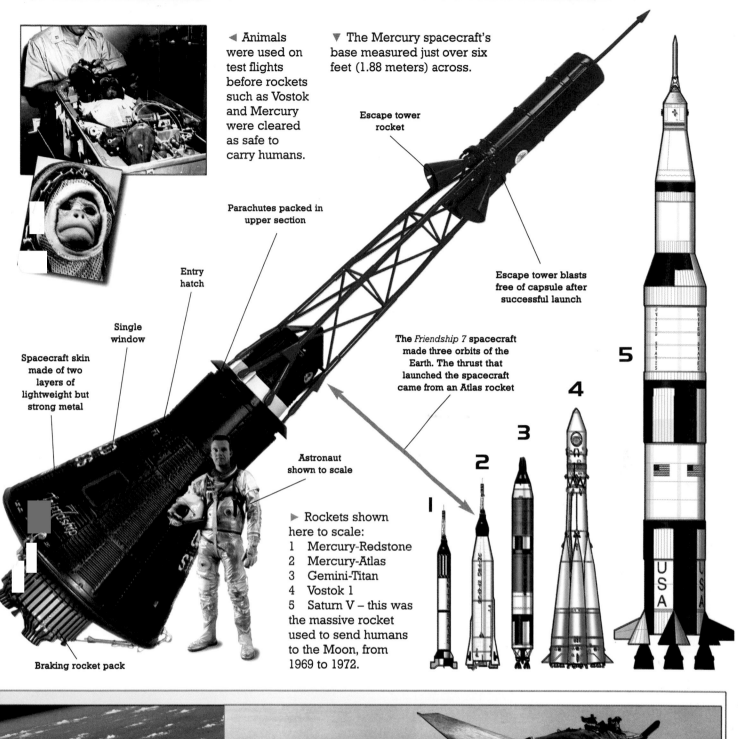

◀ Animals were used on test flights before rockets such as Vostok and Mercury were cleared as safe to carry humans.

▼ The Mercury spacecraft's base measured just over six feet (1.88 meters) across.

Escape tower rocket

Parachutes packed in upper section

Entry hatch

Single window

Spacecraft skin made of two layers of lightweight but strong metal

Escape tower blasts free of capsule after successful launch

The *Friendship 7* spacecraft made three orbits of the Earth. The thrust that launched the spacecraft came from an Atlas rocket

Astronaut shown to scale

▶ Rockets shown here to scale:
1 Mercury-Redstone
2 Mercury-Atlas
3 Gemini-Titan
4 Vostok 1
5 Saturn V – this was the massive rocket used to send humans to the Moon, from 1969 to 1972.

Braking rocket pack

▲ The X-15 was a single seater.

▲ Not all flights were successful. This one was a disaster.

RACEFACT
Eight X-15 pilots flew above 50 miles (80 kilometers). This altitude was high enough for the pilots to be called astronauts by the U.S. Air Force. Only two X-15 pilots flew to the Karman Line, which is higher still, at 62 miles (100 kilometers).

Mission training

Pioneer astronauts explored a dangerous frontier. They were trained and tested to cope with all sorts of emergencies that might occur during a mission.

The two-seat Gemini craft was the next step into space for the United States. Gemini's job was to allow astronauts to practice space maneuvers that would be needed for later missions to the Moon. Astronauts learned how to meet and link up the Gemini with other spacecraft in orbit. They also made the first space walks by American astronauts.

The life-size training rig (shown at right) allowed Gemini crews to practice how to **dock** with another spacecraft in orbit. Using the simulator, astronauts became completely familiar with the basics of a mission before they had to do it for real in space.

▲ Gemini had two hatches, one for each of the two crew members. The astronauts had to be sealed into their space suits when a hatch was opened.

▲ The **centrifuge** was an important training tool in the early days of space. It spun an astronaut around at high speed, to simulate acceleration effects.

▶ Gemini crew in a test tank, making sure they could survive after making a **splashdown**.

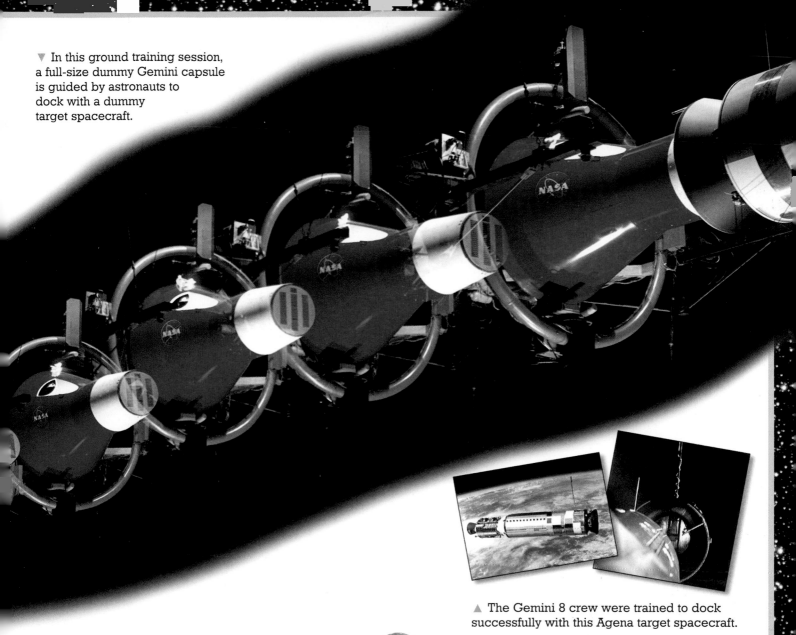

▼ In this ground training session, a full-size dummy Gemini capsule is guided by astronauts to dock with a dummy target spacecraft.

▲ The Gemini 8 crew were trained to dock successfully with this Agena target spacecraft.

What if a returning capsule went off course and landed far from help, perhaps deep in a South American jungle? To cover such an event, astronauts were given special training that taught them how to survive until rescued. Survival training is still important today, and all spacecraft carry emergency equipment.

◀ Gemini crew learn how to cope with landing in a jungle.

Space milestones

Almost every flight in the 1960s set some sort of record, as the Soviet Union and United States competed to be the leader in the space race. The ultimate target was to be the first to land humans safely on the Moon.

Among the most important space flights were those that aimed to prove spacecraft could be flown accurately in space. Two Gemini spacecraft made the first rendezvous in December 1965. They came within 12 inches (30 centimeters) of each other.

Accurate piloting was needed for this to be successful. The two spacecraft stayed close together for five hours.

A few months later, in March 1966, Gemini 8 was launched to practice docking with a target spacecraft.

RACEFACT
Early U.S. space flights always "splashed down" in the sea. Many people were involved in recovering astronauts and capsules after a mission. Gemini flights were supported by a fleet of 26 ships, 100-plus aircraft, and over 10,000 crew.

Surviving in space

Space is a deadly environment. The key to staying alive there is to wear a space suit, also called the "one-person spaceship."

The earliest space suits were developed from special suits created in the 1930s and 1940s for high-flying aviators, or pilots. Even in those days, aircraft could fly high enough to make breathing gear and body protection essential.

In space, a suit's **backpack** provides oxygen for breathing. Body heat is controlled by a cooling garment. A tough outer layer gives protection from the Sun's rays and from collisions with dust or other particles zipping through space. Radio equipment allows the astronaut to talk with controllers on Earth or in a spacecraft nearby. The arms and legs are flexible, so the wearer can move easily.

▲ American aviator Wiley Post developed the first practical suit for high flights in the 1930s.

▲ The first U.S. space walk was carried out by Ed White on the Gemini 4 mission, flown in June 1965.

◄ The first American astronauts were called the "Mercury Seven." Here they show off their aluminum-covered flight suits.

RACEFACT
Humans in space have different names, depending on the country they come from. In many countries they are known as astronauts. The Russians call them cosmonauts. The French use spacionauts, and the Chinese call them taikonauts.

▲ The Orlan's back opens like a door so a cosmonaut can climb inside easily.

◀ Helmet lights are used when the cosmonaut is in the Earth's shadow.

Death in space?

In science fiction movies such as *Total Recall* people are shown exploding in agony when exposed to the vacuum of space. Would this happen in real life?

A space suit leak is dangerous, but it is not as dramatic as in the movies. In 1965, a suit started leaking during testing in the vacuum chamber at Johnson Space Center in the U.S.

The wearer passed out through lack of air in less than half a minute, but luckily, technicians spotted the trouble. They pumped air in, and he came round without any severe problems.

It could have been much worse – low or zero air pressure can easily damage delicate body organs such as the lungs and ear drums.

Today there are several kinds of space suit. The suit above is the Russian Orlan, or the "sea eagle," which has been used since 1977. It is a "semirigid" design, with a hard body and helmet, linked to arms and legs that bend easily.

Putting on an Orlan suit is not too difficult because the backpack swings outwards to reveal a hatch the wearer uses to enter the suit. This takes only a few minutes, and the suit can keep its wearer comfortable for up to nine hours.

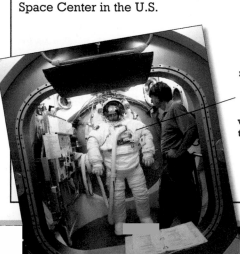

A space suit ready for testing. Air can be removed completely in a vacuum chamber, to simulate space

Reliable rocket

The Russian Soyuz rocket is a reliable spacecraft. Today's model is a more sophisticated, or improved, version of the rocket used for Gagarin's first flight.

The present-day Soyuz rocket looks much the same as the Vostok launcher that sent Yuri Gagarin into space in 1961. Although the design is over 45 years old, every part of it has been steadily improved over the years.

Soyuz has a central core stage, powered by a cluster of four motors. The core is surrounded at launch by four "strap-on" boosters, each with its own set of motors. When their fuel is used up, they drop away and the core stage carries on. The top stage provides the final shove into orbit.

▼ Soyuz rockets have made more than 1700 crewed and uncrewed flights, more than any other launcher.

Strap-on boosters fall away when their fuel is gone

Twenty rocket engines fire together at launch

▲ Soyuz rockets are carried to the launch site aboard a railway train. A powerful locomotive pulls the 30-ton (27-tonne) Soyuz along the track. When the stages are filled with fuel, the Soyuz will weigh much more – about 331 tons (300 tonnes).

Russia's space base

Russian crewed spacecraft are launched from the Baikonur **Cosmodrome** in Kazakhstan. The base was built by the Soviet Union in the 1960s as its center of space operations, and has been used ever since.

Baikonur is a good place for rocket launches because the area is flat and has few people living there. There is little chance of anyone being hurt during a launch explosion.

▶ A Soyuz soars away on the long climb to space. It can carry three cosmonauts. Supplies on board provide the crew with air, water, and food for about three days.

Rocket escape system

Crew module inside shroud

◀ Once at the launch pad, the Soyuz is slowly erected to a vertical takeoff angle, ready to be fueled for launching.

Soyuz rockets are used for both crewed and uncrewed space missions. As a space freighter, the rocket carries a Progress cargo module. For crewed flights, the three-person Soyuz crew module is carried instead. It is a system that has done well, and may be used for future flights to the Moon.

The equipment car, with diesel locomotive in front

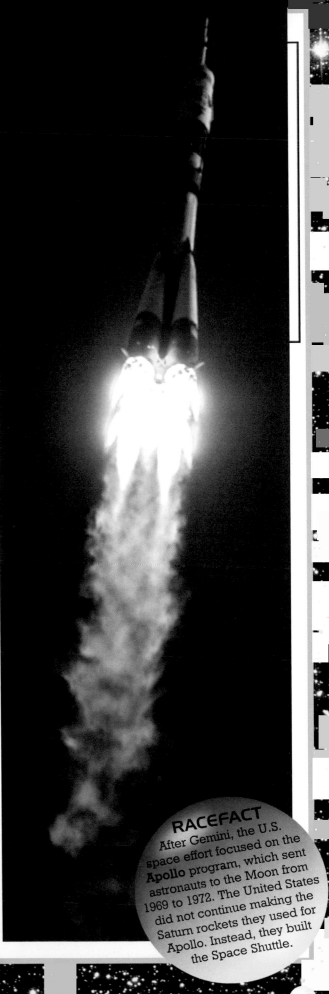

RACEFACT
After Gemini, the U.S. space effort focused on the **Apollo** program, which sent astronauts to the Moon from 1969 to 1972. The United States did not continue making the Saturn rockets they used for Apollo. Instead, they built the Space Shuttle.

◀ The heatshield of a space capsule reaches up to 5430°F (3000°C) when re-entering the atmosphere.

RACEFACT
Space capsules mostly use a heatshield made of carbon material. The outer coating melts and chars in the heat, blowing off hot gases as it does so. The gases provide a thin cushion layer between the air and the capsule, taking heat away with them.

Return to Earth

Coming down through the atmosphere is very dangerous. The biggest risk is the heat caused by the speed of re-entry.

Crewed spacecraft orbit around the Earth at nearly five miles per second (eight kilometers per second), an enormous speed that has to be reduced to almost zero just before landing. The way to do this is to use a **heatshield** that can cope with the intense heat and pressure of hitting the upper atmosphere at high speed.

To start a re-entry, a spacecraft uses braking rockets to slow down a little. Gravity then pulls the craft towards the Earth below.

Disturbed air behind capsule

Shockwave in front of capsule

Capsule shapes
The shape of a capsule affects its re-entry through the atmosphere. The Mercury capsule's shape allowed it to be steered slightly, depending on what angle it hit the upper atmosphere. Early Soviet craft, such as Vostok 1, used a non-steerable ball shape. If re-entry was set up incorrectly, the capsule could bounce off the atmosphere into space, burn up, or crash off-course.

▲ A spacecraft glows as it streaks through the upper atmosphere and super-hot air swirls past the heatshield.

▲ A helicopter hovers to pick up the crew of a U.S. space capsule.

◄ Big parachutes are needed to slow down a capsule for landing.

▼ Technicians check out a Soyuz spacecraft after a safe landing.

The last few minutes of a re-entry are when the parachutes are released. A smaller "drogue" parachute comes out first, and this pulls out the bigger main parachutes. U.S. capsules, such as the Mercury and Gemini, splashed down in the sea. Russian capsules come down on land.

The X-Prize

▲ Technicians check out SpaceShipOne before one of its test flights.

Space flight took a new turn when the X-Prize was announced in 1995. This started a new space race, between private companies, instead of governments.

The X-Prize offered $10 million to the first privately funded team that could launch a reusable manned spacecraft into space, twice in a two week period. The competition's main goal was to give a boost to low-cost space flight. The organizers thought that independent designers might be able to design and build spacecraft quicker and more cheaply than government agencies.

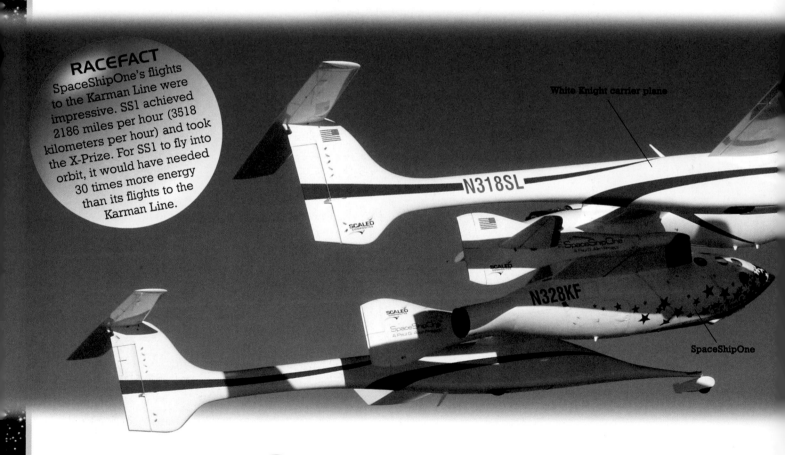

RACEFACT
SpaceShipOne's flights to the Karman Line were impressive. SS1 achieved 2186 miles per hour (3518 kilometers per hour) and took the X-Prize. For SS1 to fly into orbit, it would have needed 30 times more energy than its flights to the Karman Line.

White Knight carrier plane

N318SL

N328KF

SpaceShipOne

▲ When linked together, the White Knight and SS1 made an unlikely looking combined flying machine. White Knight has two jet engines, SS1 just a single rocket.

On October 4, 2004, nine years after the X-Prize was first offered, it was won by a tubby-looking machine called SpaceShipOne, or simply SS1. The designer, Burt Rutan, also built the White Knight carrier jet that took SS1 to a height of 8.7 miles (14 kilometers). The SS1 was then released, and pilot Brian Binnie fired its rocket motor to soar up into the sky. It reached a height above the Karman Line.

Tough rules for a ticket to space

The rules of the X-Prize, later renamed the Ansari X-Prize, were strict. To win, a team had to launch a piloted spacecraft carrying at least three crew, or a pilot plus weight equal to two people. The height flown had to be to at least 62 miles (100 kilometers).

Reaching orbital height and speed, however, was not an aim. The flight had to be repeated within two weeks by the same spacecraft.

No government money was allowed to fund development. Every entry in the competition had to be funded privately.

To measure the flights accurately, SS1 carried a flight recorder, called the "gold box," plus two other measuring systems.

▶ Here are just four X-Prize designs:
1   The Canadian Arrow is based on Wernher von Braun's V-2.
2   The Rocketplane has jet engines, to fly to base under power, rather than gliding.
3   The XF-1 is a one-seat demonstrator.
4   Starchaser is an advanced British design.

▲ When its fuel was used up, SS1 glided back to base, and landed on a long runway.

◀ The pilot's-eye view from the flight cabin of the White Knight. It has the same multi-porthole design as the SS1.

New frontiers

New technology aims to make space flight much cheaper, and easier to achieve.

▲ At first, the SS2 is attached to a carrier jet.

▶ SS2 soars to the Karman Line. Its wings go to a flip-up position, which allows the craft to re-enter at the right angle.

Plans for the future include expanding the world of private space flight. The leader in this field is Virgin Galactic. The company has big plans for SpaceShipTwo, a bigger successor to the SS1. The SS2 takes Virgin into the space tours business, with flights beyond the Karman Line for anyone who has time for a vacation and who can afford a ticket price of $200,000.

▶ SS2's passengers can now leave their seats and float around the cabin. The Earth below glows blue through the cabin's circular windows.

▼ When the soaring flight comes to an end, SS2 glides back to Earth to make a landing on the runway at its desert base.

SpaceShipTwo follows the same flight plan as SS1, starting with takeoff under a carrier jet. Following a swift climb, the SS2's rocket motor is turned off, and the spacecraft coasts for a few minutes before returning to Earth. Afterwards, the passengers receive their astronaut certificates!

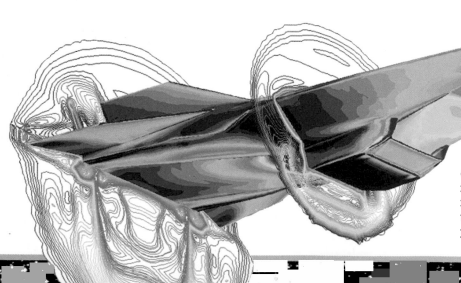

▲ By 2050, dart-shaped spacecraft like the one in this computerized image may be flying directly to space, without needing a rocket booster. A small machine based on this design has already flown at 7,000 miles per hour (11,200 kilometers per hour).

◄ Skylon could look like this before a flight. Its engines would use five times less fuel than normal rockets.

The Skylon is an idea for a future spacecraft with a new type of rocket motor. Skylon would lift off from a runway with its engines taking oxygen from the air rather than an oxidizer tank. Gradually the spacecraft would speed up to about 3300 miles per hour (5300 kilometers per hour). At this point, the engines would switch to pure rocket power for the climb to space.

▲ Cargo could be carried in Skylon's load bay. People might travel in a sealed pod, fitted with seats and life-support gear.

Space elevator

One day it may be possible to travel into space without needing a launch rocket. The plan is to develop materials that are strong enough to build a space elevator, a super-tall tower extending all the way from the ground to space. Instead of rockets, sealed elevator cars would travel up and down the tower, in a journey lasting several days. Will it ever happen? Surprisingly, it could be possible as the latest carbon materials are nearly strong enough to make such a structure.

► A future space elevator would be anchored somewhere on the **equator**. This one is positioned south of India.

Timeline

Here are discoveries and achievements marking journeys to the edge of space – from early ideas to the new world of private space flight.

▲ This postage stamp marked the 1969 Soyuz 4 and 5 space docking.

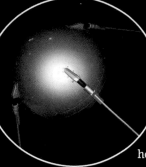

▲ Sputnik 1, the world's first artificial satellite.

About 1500 Early writings on space travel include the poem *Orlando Furioso* by Ludovico Ariosto. In this poem, Ariosto's hero goes to the Moon in a "fiery chariot."

1687 The English scientist Isaac Newton publishes *Philosophiae Naturalis Principia Mathematica* in which he describes gravity and the laws of motion. These laws explain how rockets work in a vacuum.

1783 The first hot-air and gas-filled balloon flights are made. As flights go higher, it is clear that humans need breathing gear to survive at great heights. Before this, people thought that Earth's air extended to the Moon and beyond.

1857 Konstantin Tsiolkovsky is born in Russia. He works out many basics of space flight, such as orbital speeds and multi-stage rockets. He publishes over 500 works and in 1911 writes a letter in which he says, "Earth is the cradle of humanity but one cannot live in the cradle forever."

1926 The American "father of rocketry," Robert Goddard, launches the world's first liquid-fuel rocket. By 1935, his rockets have flown at 550 miles per hour (885 kilometers per hour).

1942 The first test launches of the V-2 rocket weapon are made under the direction of German scientist Wernher von Braun. Von Braun would later become famous for leading the U.S. space program during the space race with the Soviet Union.

1957 The world's first artificial satellite is launched in October by the Soviet Union. Sputnik 1 weighs 184 pounds (83.6 kilograms) and orbits the Earth every 96 minutes. In November, Sputnik 2 carries the dog Laika, the first living thing in orbit.

1958 The National Aeronautics and Space Administration (NASA) is founded in the U.S.

1959 The first flight of the X-15 rocket plane. Three are built and make 199 flights between them until 1968, although one is lost in an accident. The highest flight reached was almost 67 miles (108 kilometers) with Joe Walker at the controls.

▲ Sergei Korolev, the man in charge of designing early Soviet spacecraft.

1960 Wernher von Braun is placed in charge of U.S. space rocket development.

1961 On April 12, Yuri Gagarin becomes the first human in space, making a single orbit of the Earth in the spacecraft Vostok 1.

1961 On May 5, Mercury spacecraft *Freedom 7* carries Alan Shepard Jr. above the Karman Line.

1962 On February 20, Mercury *Friendship 7* carries John Glenn into space. He orbits the Earth three times.

1963 Soviet cosmonaut Valentina Tereshkova flies aboard Vostok 6 to become the first woman in space. She orbits the Earth 48 times.

1965 Cosmonaut Aleksei Leonov carries out the first space walk outside the spacecraft Voskhod 2. The walk lasts 20 minutes.

► In a major emergency, the Mercury spacecraft's escape tower could lift the capsule free of the launch rocket in less than a second.

1965 Various landmarks in space history are made by Gemini spacecraft. The first crewed Gemini mission is flown by astronauts Virgil "Gus" Grissom and John Young, who orbit the Earth three times. In June, Ed White makes the first U.S. space walk from Gemini 4, which lasts for 22 minutes. In December, Gemini 7 makes 206 orbits, proving that humans can stay alive in space long enough to make a future trip to the Moon. Also in December, Gemini 6 and 7 make the first space rendezvous.

1966 U.S. spacecraft Gemini 8 makes the first docking with another spacecraft, an uncrewed Agena target vehicle.

1967 The Soviet Soyuz 1 is launched, carrying Vladimir Komarov. It returns to Earth on April 24, but the parachute gets tangled in mid-air. Komarov is killed in the crash. He is the first human to die while on a space mission. Earlier the same year, three U.S. astronauts died while their rocket was still on the launch pad.

1968 The first humans leave Earth orbit. The crew of Apollo 8 fly around the Moon, but do not attempt to land there.

1969 In January, Soyuz 4 and 5 carry out the first Soviet space docking. Cosmonauts move between the two craft.

1969 On July 20, Neil Armstrong and Buzz Aldrin become the first humans to set foot on the Moon, after landing their Apollo 11 Lunar Module (LM) safely on the Moon.

1969-1972 Apollo 11 is followed by further successful landings, by Apollos 12, 14, 15, and 16. Apollo 17 of December 1972 was the last mission to the Moon – no humans have been there since.

1973 The U.S. sends no more flights to the Moon. Instead, the crewed Space Shuttle is developed only for flights to and from Earth orbit. The Soviet Union flies no cosmonauts to the Moon, also concentrating on space missions in Earth orbit.

▶ The Burt Rutan-designed SpaceShipOne (top), compared with the bigger SpaceShipTwo, designed to carry two crew plus six passengers to the edge of space.

1995 The X-Prize is a $10-million competition launched by Peter Diamandis. Its aim is to spur the development of private spacecraft to take humans to the edge of space. The X-Prize is similar to prizes offered in aviation's early years, such as the $25,000 Orteig Prize that inspired Charles Lindbergh to fly across the Atlantic Ocean in 1927.

2004 SpaceShipOne makes its first flight in June. U.S. designer Burt Rutan created a two-craft system that includes the White Knight carrier plane. This takes SS1 high into the air, before it is dropped and the rocket motor is switched on. On 4 October, SS1 flies past the Karman Line to take the Ansari X-Prize.

2008 The first planned flights of the Virgin Galactic spaceline. SpaceShipTwo has a top speed of about 2500 miles per hour (4000 kilometers per hour).

▲ Front view of the White Knight jet plane, used to carry SpaceShipOne.

▲ Vostok 1, Yuri Gagarin's spacecraft. The rear section (arrowed) is the third stage of the launch rocket. It parted from the capsule in orbit.

▼ SpaceDev is another private space pioneer, with this six-seater, called the Dream Chaser.

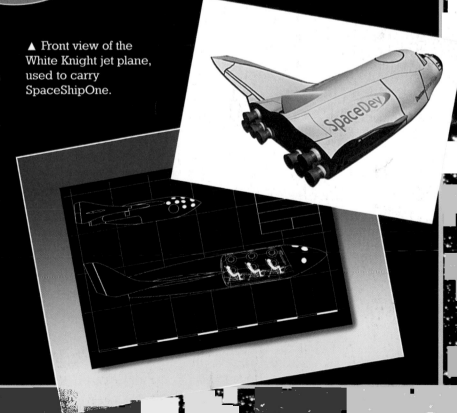

Glossary

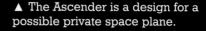

Here are explanations of many of the terms used in this book.

▲ The Ascender is a design for a possible private space plane.

▲ This rocket test shows hot gases roaring out of the nozzle. The combustion chamber is above it.

Antenna A rod or dish-shaped aerial that transmits or receives radio and TV signals.

Apollo The NASA space program that took humans to the Moon from 1969 to 1972.

Atmosphere The blanket of gases that surrounds the Earth. It is a mixture of gases, mostly nitrogen and oxygen.

Aurora A glow seen in the night sky, often near the poles. It looks like moving curtains of light. Auroras are electrical, caused by colliding particles in the upper atmosphere.

Backpack Part of a space suit that holds life-support gear, such as breathing, cooling, and power equipment.

Booster Rocket One or more extra rockets that increase the lifting abilities of the main rocket at takeoff. They drop away when their fuel is used up.

Braking rocket Any rocket motor that is used to slow down a spacecraft.

Centrifuge A large spinning machine used to test astronauts with acceleration forces above those of the normal 1 G of Earth's gravity.

Combustion chamber Part of a rocket motor where fuel is burned. The hot gases produce thrust when directed out of the rocket nozzle.

Cosmodrome Russian name for their launch pad facilities, especially at Baikonur in Central Asia.

Dock Describes two spacecraft linking together. Crewed craft have a hatchway so that astronauts can move between one spacecraft and another.

Equator An imaginary circle drawn around the Earth, halfway between the poles. The equator divides our planet into a Northern Hemisphere and a Southern Hemisphere.

Gravity The force of attraction between objects. The pull of gravity at the Earth's surface is 1G, but astronauts typically feel about 4G during a rocket takeoff, and are weightless in orbit.

Heatshield Protection for a spacecraft re-entering the atmosphere after a space mission.

Hubble Space Telescope (HST) A truck-sized satellite that was launched in 1990 by the crewed U.S. Space Shuttle. It orbits far above the atmosphere so its instruments are not affected by the dust or pollution in the Earth's atmosphere.

International Space Station (ISS) A crewed research base being built in orbit. It is a project between the U.S., Russia, Japan, Canada, and Europe, plus many smaller contributors. The ISS orbits about 220 miles (350 kilometers) above Earth.

Karman Line The boundary between air and space, named after Hungarian-American physicist Theodore von Karman (1881-1963). He first worked out that at 62 miles (100 kilometers) up, the air is too thin for an aircraft to fly. The height is accepted by the Fédération Aéronautique Internationale (FAI), which sets such rules and standards.

Liquid-fuel rocket An engine that works by burning a liquid, such as kerosene, with an oxidizer, such as liquid oxygen.

Meteor A chunk of space dust or rock that enters the atmosphere and glows brightly with heat as it burns up in the upper atmosphere. Some meteors are not destroyed entirely and hit the ground as a meteorite, sometimes blasting out an impact crater.

Module A section of a spacecraft. Examples are crew, cargo, or communications modules.

Orbit The curving path a space object takes around another. The Earth orbits the Sun once a year, while the Moon orbits the Earth every 27.3 days. The artificial satellite Sputnik 1 orbited the Earth once every 96 minutes.

Oxidizer A substance that allows a fuel to burn when they are mixed. The most common oxidizer is liquid oxygen, which can be mixed with various fuels including kerosene or liquid hydrogen.

► Gemini astronaut Ed White performs a space walk high above the Earth. He had no backpack with life-support equipment on this space walk. Instead, air was pumped to his suit through a long snaking pipe, called an umbilical.

Oxygen A common chemical element found in rocks and as a gas in the air we breathe. Earth's atmosphere contains 21 percent oxygen, the rest is mostly nitrogen gas.

Re-entry Coming back into the Earth's atmosphere after a space mission. The extreme heat caused by hitting the air at high speed means that a spacecraft must have some form of heatshield protection.

Satellite A space object that orbits another. The Moon is Earth's natural satellite, but there are thousands of human-made artificial satellites.

Solid-fuel rocket A rocket that works like a firework, burning a solid mix of fuel and oxidizer.

Soviet Union A group of 15 states that existed in Eastern Europe and Asia. From 1945 until 1991 it was one of the world's two superpowers along with the United States. The Soviet Union collapsed in 1991. The 15 states are now separate countries.

Space plane A spacecraft with wings, rather than a capsule shape.

Space Shuttle NASA's crewed rocket system that has been used since the early 1980s. It consists of an Orbiter space plane, a huge fuel tank and two rocket boosters.

Space walk A person floating in space outside a spacecraft, wearing a space suit.

Splashdown The name for the U.S. style of landing crewed capsules in the ocean, for recovery by ships and helicopters.

Stage A section of a rocket which drops away when its fuel is used up, after which the next stage takes over. Stage rockets come in many designs, with two, three, or four stages.

Thrust The force that pushes an aircraft forward.

Turbopump A powerful pump designed to force fuel and oxidizer into a rocket's combustion chamber at very high pressure.

Vacuum Somewhere empty of matter, so that there is no air there.

World War II An international conflict that lasted from 1939 to 1945.

▲ A Soyuz rocket, fueled up and ready for flight. The four boosters can be seen around the rocket's base.

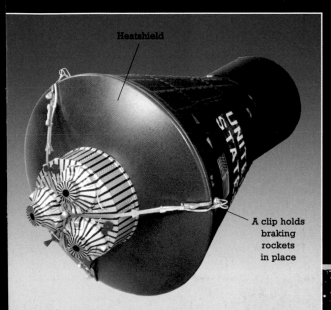

Heatshield

A clip holds braking rockets in place

◄ The Mercury's spacecraft had three braking rockets held to the base by cable connectors. In the first minutes of re-entry, heat burned through the cables and the braking pack fell away. The heatshield then protected the spacecraft through the rest of re-entry.

Index

Acknowledgements
We wish to thank all those people who
have helped to create this publication.
Information and images were supplied
by:
Individuals:
    D. Ducros/ESA
    Mat Irvine/Smallspace Photos
    iStockphoto/Penfold, Stephen Sweet
    David Jefferis
    Gavin Page/Design Shop
Organizations:
    Alpha Archive
    Bristol Spaceplanes Ltd
    Canadian Arrow/PlanetSpace
    DreamSpace Group/Da Vinci
        Project
    Energia Corporation
    ESA European Space Agency
    JPL Jet Propulsion Laboratory
    Konstantin E. Tsiolkovsky, State
        Museum of the History of
        Cosmonautics
    NASA Space Agency
    Novosti Agency
    Reaction Engines Ltd
    Rocketplane Kistler
    RSC Energia Corporation
    Scaled Composites, LLC
    Science Museum, London
    Starchaser Industries Ltd
    Virgin Galactic Spaceline

Printed in the U.S.A.